JAPAN

FOR

FIRST TIME

TRAVELERS

*Everything You Need to Know
Before You Go*

MONICA FRICKS

Japan For First Time Travelers
Everything You Need to Know Before You Go

Copyright © Monica Fricks

All rights reserved. No part of this publication may be reproduced, distributed, or transmitted in any form or by any means, including photocopying, recording, or other electronic or mechanical methods, without the prior written permission of the author, except in the case of brief quotations embodied in critical reviews and certain other noncommercial uses permitted by copyright law. For permission requests, write to the author, addressed "Attention: Permissions Coordinator," at www.japanalytic.com.

ISBN (paperback): 978-1-7365754-0-6

Cover image is the property of Monica Fricks and may not be reproduced or used without prior written permission.

First edition 2021.

TABLE OF CONTENTS

Introduction   4

Part 1: Preparations and Planning   5

Deciding When You Want to Go   6
Deciding Where You Want to Go   8
Money-saving Tips   12
Booking Accommodations   21
What to Pack   24

Part 2: Good Things to Know for Worry-free Travel   30

Travel Rules and Restrictions   31
Health and Safety   34
Basic Japanese Culture Tips   37

Part 3: Answers to Frequently Asked Questions from First Time Travelers to Japan   41

Part 4: Helpful Links   50

Introduction

This book is designed as a quick guide for travelers who have never been to Japan. Everything included has been put to the test on numerous trips. Inside, there are basic planning tips, travel suggestions, and important things to know once you're there to help make your time in Japan as worry-free as possible.

You will also find "Pro Tips" at the end of each section. These information-packed segments give you helpful tips from seasoned Japan travelers on things you won't find in other travel books.

Note to Readers

Portions of this book are taken from the author's Japanalytic™ blog. So if you want to read more on a particular subject, get travel ideas, or just read interesting things about Japan, check out **www.japanalytic.com**.

Follow Us!

You can also follow Japanalytic™ on social media. We post daily!

- Instagram: **@japanalytic**
- Facebook: **facebook.com/japanalytic**

PREPARATIONS & PLANNING

Deciding When You Want to Go

Pick a Time that Fits Your Budget
Just like any other vacation spot, Japan has peak travel seasons when prices are higher. Peak seasons in Japan are early March to mid-May, and early October to late November. So if cost is a concern, it's best to look for travel dates outside those months.

Decide What Weather You Want
Weather impacts not only what you'll have to pack, but also what activities you'll be able to do. Some parts of Japan like Kyoto have rainy seasons, while other places like Sapporo have cold winters. So, weather preferences and the types of outdoor activities you like to do should definitely be taken into consideration when planning your visit.

Decide What Activities You Want to Do
Your activity preferences also impact when you should go to Japan. For instance, if you really want to hike Mount Fuji, part of your visit will need to be from 1 July – 14 September, because Fuji's hiking trails are only open during that time.

Another thing to check for Mount Fuji (and many mountains in Japan) is the Volcanic Alert Level. Because Fuji is an active volcano, sometimes the concentration of volcanic gases is high and Japanese authorities shut down public access to trails and the cable car ride, the Mount Fuji Panoramic Ropeway. You can check Japan's official website for Mount Fuji conditions at www.fujisan-climb.jp.

It's always a good idea to make sure the attraction you plan to visit is open prior to going. In addition to environmental factors that can happen at any time, many of Japan's attractions are closed on Mondays.

Pro Tip

It's a good idea to have Japanese Yen with you at all times. Ideally, you should carry enough to cover all of your daily activities. While more and more businesses are accepting credit cards, many places in Japan are still cash-only, especially in small towns and rural areas.

Deciding Where You Want to Go

Planning a trip to a place as far away as Japan can seem a bit overwhelming, but it doesn't have to! Just remember that even the best-laid plans can change, and that's ok. Having a basic outline of your trip with at least a few ideas about where you want to go, can really help take the stress out of your travel, even if your itinerary changes.

Decide What's Important to You

Everybody has preferences, and it's no different when you travel. Some people want to visit cultural sites, while others prefer outdoor activities like hiking. In order to plan for Japan, decide what you enjoy most, then pick your travel destinations accordingly.

Most big cities have a little bit of everything, but some locations are better choices for specific interests. For example, Kyoto has a very traditional feel and is known for its temples and cultural sites, while Sapporo is known for its wide-open natural spaces, outdoor activities and winter snowfall.

If you have limited time but want to experience a little bit of everything, Tokyo is a great place to see both modern and ancient. Tokyo's Robot Restaurant and the Studio Ghibli Museum are great places to experience modern Japan, but at Senso-ji Temple in Asakusa, you'll step back into the past. The temple was completed in the year 645.

Figure Out What You Enjoy Most

While most of us know what we like to do when we travel, it may be necessary to decide what you enjoy most, especially if you'll have only a short stay in Japan. Deciding ahead of time what your travel priorities are will help you decide where to go with the time you have. (And remember to be realistic about travel times and give yourself plenty of time to enjoy each site.)

In big cities like Tokyo, you can get more done if you group a day's activities based on location. In other words, if you choose activities that are close together and visit them in the same day, you'll spend less time traveling back and forth.

Weigh the Pros and Cons

Sometimes it's hard to decide between trip activities, but one thing that can help is to weigh the pros and cons. For example, let's say you're traveling in December and you've decided you really want to see Matsumoto Castle in Nagano because it's one of Japan's national treasures, but you don't like cold weather.

Nagano is very cold in the Winter (in fact it's part of Japan's "snow country" and even hosted the 1998 Winter Olympics). So in this case, checking out Shuri Castle Park, a World Heritage Site in Naha, Okinawa, may suit your travel preferences better this time because it's warm there year-round. Okinawa is also known for its eclectic cuisine, Chinese influenced-architecture and world-class scuba diving.

Pick Which Cities You Want to Visit
Deciding which cities to visit can also be a tough decision because each has its own unique draw. To choose, look at the main attractions for each city and factor in weather, travel time and cost. Budget and the time are usually the most important factors in figuring out where you can go.

Research Events and Festivals
Japan has festivals (called *matsuri*) year-round, and every region has its own unique celebration. Some festivals are more popular than others, and this can affect crowds and prices. One of the biggest festivals in Japan is Gion Matsuri, held in July in Kyoto. During this festival, area hotel rates are higher (and rooms book quickly). However, despite the cost, it's the most popular festival in Japan and you're almost guaranteed to see geisha.

Give Yourself Free Time to Relax or Explore
This is a very important step in any trip. Feeling rushed or stressed can really take away from the enjoyment of travel, so be sure not to pack your daily schedule with too many activities. Leaving some free time in your day can also allow you to explore and experience Japanese culture more deeply. With a few exceptions, quality over quantity is usually the way to go.

Have a Backup Plan

Even the most well thought out plans can change - and that's ok! Flexibility is a key ingredient in any travel itinerary and having an alternate plan can really help ease the stress of any travel-related hiccups. For example, if you planned to hike Mount Fuji but the trail gets closed, you could always check out Mount Takao instead. It's about an hour away from Tokyo's city center and is a beautifully forested, peaceful hike with great views from its summit.

Pro Tip

Japan's train stations usually have multiple exits and some of those exits (like the ones in Tokyo and Ginza stations) can be pretty far apart. Figuring out which exit is closest to your destination can help save you a lot of time and walking.

You can either use maps posted in the stations (though some may not be in English) or even better, pre-plan your route. Many stations have English language floor plans posted online.

Money-Saving Tips

One of the few downsides about traveling to Japan is that it can be expensive. Here are some simple tips that can save you big bucks.

Travel Off-Season

Traveling to Japan during major festivals, Golden Week, or peak season (such as when the cherry blossoms bloom), can mean higher prices. If cost is a concern, consider traveling during the off-season and avoid travel dates that coincide with major festivals.

In large cities like Tokyo and Kyoto, cherry blossoms typically bloom in late March or early April. Golden Week, which is a week filled with several Japanese holidays, is from April 29th – May 5th.

Stay at a Ryokan, Hostel or Capsule Hotel

Lodging can be one of the most expensive parts of any trip. Cheaper options for the traveler on a budget are: Japanese-style inns (called *ryokan*), hostels, and capsule hotels (usually just a private bed similar to a train berth, though some offer slightly larger rooms). Don't expect spacious accommodations or a western-style stay, but that's part of the fun!

If you decide to try one of Japan's unique capsule hotels, be aware that most are men-only, so be sure to check hotel policies prior to booking. There are increasingly more women-only capsule hotels each year, and two of the most popular in Tokyo are Akihabara's Bay Hotel and Nine Hours in Shinjuku.

Look for Hotel Discounts

When booking your trip, look for discounted hotel rates. Booking sites often run specials in the off-season. During peak season, look for package deals on those sites instead. Customer reviews and photos can also really help you select a budget-friendly hotel without sacrificing quality.

Choose Low-cost Sightseeing Activities

Some of Japan's most interesting and beautiful spots offer cheap or even free admission. For example, Tokyo's Imperial Palace East Gardens are free. These gardens are filled with perfectly manicured bonsai trees and have great views of the Imperial Palace.

If you decide to go to the gardens, another great place to check out on the way is Tokyo Station itself. Once you get to the station, walk to the Marunouchi Central Gate exit. This exit is closest to the palace and offers great views of Tokyo Station's iconic architecture.

The building was completed in 1914 and its unique domes really stand out among the surrounding skyscrapers. Inside Tokyo Station, you'll also find "Kitchen Street", which is packed with all kinds of budget-friendly eateries. For a Tokyo train station map, go to www.jreast.co/jp/e/stations.

Another budget-friendly place to check out is Toyosu Fish Market. It's one of the busiest fish markets in the world and they don't charge admission. Neighboring Harajuku and Yoyogi Park are also free and have some of the best, uniquely Japanese entertainment you'll find. On weekends, the area is flooded with cosplayers dressed in their best, and they usually love to pose for pictures. Harajuku is also packed with budget-friendly stores and restaurants.

Get Out and Walk

Transportation fees can really add up, especially in big cities like Tokyo. You can save money on transportation by walking to your destination when it's feasible. Many travelers report some of their most interesting and uniquely Japanese experiences happened when they were walking around exploring. And the best thing is, it's entirely free to sightsee on foot!

Shop at Markets and Low-Cost Souvenir Stores

To find budget-friendly souvenirs, shop at the local market. Every city has at least one. For instance, Nishiki Market in Kyoto is a great spot for a wide variety of unique, budget-friendly items (and there's even a Japanese sword store).

Temples and shrines, like Yasaka Shrine in Kyoto, also sometimes have little markets set up with food and souvenirs. Be aware though, that some markets are only open on certain days so planning ahead is necessary.

While Tokyo can be an expensive place to shop, you *can* find low-cost, high-quality souvenirs. Two of the best spots are Harajuku's Daiso (a popular store where everything is 100 yen (approximately 1 USD)), and Oriental Bazaar in Omotesando.

Eat at Noodle Stands, Curry Shops, Konbini & Department Stores

Because many Japanese commute to the city for work, they eat away from home a lot. As a result, you'll find a wide variety of low cost eateries that offer lunch and dinner specials. Some of the best places to eat on a budget are noodle and curry shops, and they're plentiful in most Japanese cities. These shops offer low cost, delicious dishes, usually in large quantities.

Another great option you can find almost anywhere in Japan is the convenience store. Known as *konbini*, these stores have delicious, fresh foods like sandwiches, salads, and even hot dishes you can grab and go.

Many locals also take advantage of department store food halls (called *depachika*). Japanese department stores have a huge selection of fresh food, and it goes on sale every evening about an hour before closing time. Because there are so many options and you can get small portions, department stores are a great way to sample a wide variety of only-in-Japan foods.

Food halls are typically found on the basement levels of department stores, and there are usually plenty of places to sit and eat. Great places to try are Solamachi, which is located under the Toyko Skytree, and Shinjuku's Takashimaya. There are also Takashimaya locations in Kyoto, Osaka and Yokohama.

Get your Sushi from a Fish Market or Kaiten

While sushi is a must for most travelers, it can be expensive, even in Japan. Luckily there are budget-friendly options. Some of the cheapest (and freshest) sushi comes from stalls in fish markets. Vendors offer a nice variety and often hand roll the sushi right in front of you. Tsukiji and Toyosu markets in Tokyo, and Nishiki Market in Kyoto, are excellent spots for fresh sushi.

If you don't plan to visit a market, you can also try a conveyor belt sushi restaurant (called *kaiten*). They offer a wide variety of sushi and a fun experience at low prices. One of Tokyo's most popular kaiten chains is Ganso Zushi.

Get Out of Tokyo

While Tokyo is fascinating and absolutely worth a visit, it is also one of Japan's most expensive cities. Staying in other cities and towns for lower-cost lodging, food and souvenirs can really help you save money. The bullet train (*shinkansen*) links Tokyo to cities all over Japan's main island of Honshu with a comfortable and relatively quick trip.

Yokohama and Hachioji are great alternatives to Tokyo city center where you can usually find cheaper lodging.

Enjoy Nightlife at an Izakaya

Evening entertainment can be expensive. For a fun, low-cost experience, head to an izakaya. Izakaya are popular with locals for their cheap eats and lively atmosphere (and sometimes their karaoke). The Ebisu area of Tokyo is known for its numerous izakaya.

Two of the most popular are Ebisu Kura and Ebisu Dedesuke, which both serve Japanese-style food (*washoku*). Just look for the red lanterns that hang outside izakaya entrances and go on in.

Get Your Discount Rail Pass

If you plan to travel by train, especially cross-country, check into a JR Pass. This pass allows you unlimited travel on the bullet trains (*shinkansen*), and lets you ride many of the local trains run by JR. Passes can be purchased for increments of 1 week, 2 weeks or 3 weeks.

Here are four important things to know about the JR Pass: 1) Passes must be purchased **before** you arrive in Japan (and you will be sent a hard copy voucher, so give yourself time to receive it); 2) you must have your passport with you in order to exchange your voucher; 3) make the exchange when you're ready to use your pass, because once the voucher is exchanged, your pass is activated (so be sure your

1-week, 2-week or 3-week pass will cover the time you plan to travel by shinkansen); and, 4) not all stations have exchange offices. Narita Airport, Tokyo Station and Kyoto Station are a few of the places you can make the exchange.

The amount of long distance train travel you plan to do will determine whether the price of a JR Pass makes sense for you. Go to jrailpass.com for more information.

Use Budget Airlines

If you plan to travel long distances or visit more than one island in Japan, check out discount airlines. Domestic carriers like Peach, Jetstar and Skymark typically charge a fraction of the fare you would pay with other airlines.

Be sure to check baggage policies though, because some airlines charge extra for checked bags, and the bags you are allowed to carry on must be pretty small and light (and they do get weighed prior to you boarding).

Book a Round Trip Train Ticket
If you're flying in and out of Narita Airport and plan to take the JR Narita Express train (N'EX) or the Keisei Skyliner express train into Tokyo, booking a round trip ticket to and from the airport (vice booking a one-way ticket each time) will save you money.

The Keisei Skyliner goes into Tokyo's Ueno Station (on the east side of the city), and N'EX goes into the following Tokyo stations: Ikebukuro, Shinjuku, Shibuya, Shinagawa and Tokyo. You can purchase tickets for both trains at Terminals 1 and 2 in Narita Airport. Each takes about 40 minutes.

Keisei also offers local train service from Narita Airport. It's a good bit cheaper, but also makes frequent stops and takes about an an hour and a half to 2 hours to get into Tokyo.

Pro Tip
Many attractions are closed on Mondays. However, if Monday is a national holiday, the attraction will typically be open, and then closed the following day instead. So when planning your trip, be sure to check open days of the attractions you want to visit.

Pro Tip

In Japan, rail maps are prominently displayed by ticket kiosks and often have both Japanese and English versions. However, sometimes the English language map doesn't list fares.

If this happens, you can figure out a fare by counting the number of stops to your destination using the English language map, and then counting the same number of stops on the Japanese language map. (Just be sure to use the same color rail line and count the stops in the same direction.) Then, pay the fare shown for the stop you're headed to.

If you end up paying the wrong fare, don't worry. There are fare adjustment machines next to station exit turnstiles.

You can also purchase a pre-paid card to take the guesswork out of fares. Check out the FAQ section for more details.

Pro Tip

If you're having trouble remembering the different sections of Tokyo or deciding which station to use, pull up the a map of the Yamanote Line for reference. It's got most of Tokyo's wards included in its 29 stops.

Booking Accommodations

Determine Your Priorities
The best way to decide where to stay in Japan is much like anywhere else. It's based on hotel cost, location and amenities. In Tokyo, lodging is a little pricey overall, and you'll generally pay more to stay in the city center or in ritzy sections like Ginza.

Sometimes you can save time and money by staying outside a major city and choosing lodging close to an attraction you want to visit. For instance, if you plan to visit Mt. Fuji, lodging in the nearby mountainside town of Hakone is usually cheaper than Tokyo.

Hakone is a great way to experience small-town Japan, and is famous for its hot springs (called *onsen*). So if you were planning to check out Japan's public baths, or just need some time to relax, Hakone is a great place to do it.

If you're having trouble deciding where to stay, pictures and customer reviews can help you narrow it down.

See What's Included
Some Japanese hotels throw in freebies to draw customers. They often include things like breakfast and Wi-Fi, which can be real money savers. Others offer free shuttles to train stations or nearby attractions, and a few even provide free shuttles from Narita

Airport to Tokyo (which is about 45 miles (72km) away!).

So checking into amenities and inclusions can really make a difference in both convenience and cost. You can find information on amenities and inclusions on the booking or hotel website.

Check Cancellation Policies Prior to Booking

Many Japanese hotels allow full refunds if canceled within 24 hours, but some either don't offer cancellation at all or charge more to have the opportunity to cancel, should the need arise. Again, it's best to check.

Check Hotel Notices

For the best possible experience, check for notices of construction or unavailability of amenities (such as pool or gym closure) that will occur during your stay. Booking websites usually have these notices, but it's best to check the hotel website for the latest information.

Booking

To book a room in Japan, it's usually easiest to use a booking website. You can sometimes get a better rate if you call a hotel directly, but with the exception of major hotels, you may have trouble finding an English speaker (especially outside of Tokyo). Reservations typically open a year in advance, so to get the exact time and place you want, book as early as possible.

Take Hard Copies of Your Reservation Details

With international travel, having hard copies of your reservations is a good idea. This way, if your smart device can't connect, or if the hotel or booking sites are down, you'll be able to show the hotel staff proof of your reservation.

Many of the booking sites also include a Japanese translation of your reservation details that can help simplify the check in process. You can also show your hotel information to your taxi driver if there's a language barrier.

You'll also need your lodging details for the information card you provide to Immigration when you arrive in Japan, so having that information handy is a huge help then too!

Pro Tip
In an effort to go green, many Japanese train stations don't offer paper towels or hand dryers, so it's a good idea to carry a hand towel with you on your travels. If you forget to bring one, you can usually find them for sale in convenience stores and train stations. They're great low-cost souvenirs too, as most have Japanese designs and are under 800 Yen (about 8 USD).

What to Pack

What you pack is a very personal decision, because what one person considers unimportant, another may see as absolutely essential. So while Japan does have unique experiences you need to pack for, what you bring will still largely be based on personal preference. Here are some general guidelines that will help you bring what you need and leave what you don't.

Plan for All Types of Weather

As with any trip, where you plan to travel should determine what you pack. Because Japan is a long chain of islands running north-south, it has several climate zones and a wide variety of weather. So it's a good idea to check the average temperatures and typical weather of your destination during the month(s) you will travel.

For example, many travelers might not know Kyoto can get snow in the winter and has a rainy season in the summer. Tokyo can also get pretty rainy during several months of the year. It's also a good idea to check forecasts right before your departure date, so you're prepared for any abnormal weather you might encounter.

Pack for the Activities You Have Planned

Bring clothes and shoes appropriate for the locations and activities on your travel list. (For example, if you plan to go to a water park, bring a bathing suit!) To help save space in your suitcase and prevent overweight baggage fees, try and bring versatile items that can be used with several outfits and layered if necessary.

Try to Pack Light and Use Small Rolling Luggage

The vast majority of travelers will use public transportation to get around Japan. Because space is limited and train cars can get crowded, luggage can be annoying for you and others. Most trains, including the cross-country bullet trains (*shinkansen*), have limited overhead space that is designed for smaller bags.

If you do bring a large bag, you will probably have to hold it (usually in the walkway), as overhead racks are quite small. The Narita Express train (N'EX) connecting Narita Airport and Tokyo is one of the few trains equipped for large luggage. Shinkansen have a small area behind the last row of seats that can accommodate large bags, but it can fill up fast.

Whatever bag you decide to bring, make sure it has wheels. You will be surprised at the amount of walking (and stairs) you'll do in Japan, even in airports and train stations. You certainly don't want to have to carry even a small suitcase over long distances.

Bring Good Shoes

Whether you plan to tour mountainside temples or sightsee in a city, your feet will get a workout. Japanese train stations can be huge and taxis are often expensive, so it's best to come prepared to walk. In addition to being comfortable, your shoes should have good tread, especially if you plan to explore temple sites. Temples and shrines are often on hillsides, where footing can be uneven and outdoor steps can get slippery.

Electronics, Chargers, and Converters/Adaptors

Japan uses 100V and 2-pronged sockets. While most North American electronics (which use 120V and usually 2-pronged plugs) will work in Japan, some appliances like curling irons and hairdryers can cause problems, so it's still a good idea to bring a converter and adaptor. This is especially true if you plan to travel to smaller towns, because their electrical systems can be a bit dated. Residents of countries outside North America usually need converters and adaptors.

If you forget to bring an electronics-related item, Akihabara (also known as Akiba and "Electric Town") is a great place to find it. The shops outside Tokyo's Akihabara Station have huge selections and prices are generally good. Just bring the cord, device, or even a picture of what you need, and one of the shop attendants will almost certainly find what you're looking for, no Japanese necessary.

Akihabara is also a great place to get photo batteries, memory cards and anything related to anime. To get to Akihabara Station, you can take either the JR Yamanote Line or the Tokyo Metro Hibiya Line.

Translator/Dictionary

Because few travelers speak Japanese and many Japanese outside of Tokyo don't speak much English, it's best to bring an English-Japanese dictionary or translator. You can either bring a hardcopy version or save space in your suitcase by downloading an app to your smartphone.

If you choose the hardcopy, several publishers offer pocket-sized dictionaries with key phrases you'll need during your trip. If you plan to use an app, be sure to download it prior to your travel to ensure you have the memory and it uploads successfully. (Also make sure the app you choose will work in Japan.)

Two of the most popular translator apps are Imiwa and Papago. Imiwa is a Japanese-English dictionary app that works offline (so it's great to have in a pinch), while Papago translates voice, text and images, but requires an internet connection. Both are free.

Bring a Few Small Souvenirs from Your Hometown

In Japanese culture, souvenirs or *omiyage*, are given as ways to say thank you. While gifts are not required or expected during your travel in Japan, having a small but meaningful gift can be a great way to say thank you or express appreciation.

For example, if you plan to have a meal with a Japanese family, or if socializing with locals is big on your to-do list, bring a few trinkets to give them. Ideal gifts are something specific to your country or town, small, and not too expensive. Simple gifts like magnets, bottle openers or candies are usually good ideas.

Business Travelers Need Conservative Clothes & Business Cards

Professionals in Japan dress conservatively and formally. A suit is expected for both men and women and dark colors are preferred. Most dry cleaners in Japan offer same or next day service and many hotels will handle dry cleaning and laundry for you for a fee.

Another thing business travelers cannot forget is business cards (*meishi*). These are absolutely crucial at any Japanese meeting, and are used to help introduce the group. Every Japanese at the meeting will have a business card for you, and each will expect one in return. It's also a good idea to have a business card organizer (even if you purchase one just for your trip), because how you treat someone's business card is taken very personally (and most Japanese will have an organizer).

Medications

Be sure to bring enough medication to last the duration of your trip, with a little extra just in case. It's best to transport your medicine in the prescription bottles they came in, because the bottle shows both the name of the medication and that the medicine is prescribed to you, which should help avoid any issues at Customs.

Pro Tip

If you discover you forgot to pack something, you can probably find it in a convenience store. Japanese convenience stores (*konbini*) carry a wide variety of items like toiletries, socks and even umbrellas (*kasa*) for low prices.

Japan's major convenience stores are Lawson, Family Mart, 7-Eleven and Circle K Sunkus. They're plentiful, easy to find, and open 24/7.

GOOD THINGS TO KNOW FOR WORRY-FREE TRAVEL

Travel Rules and Restrictions

Laws and travel regulations vary from country to country. So for your trip to Japan, it's a good idea to know a little about some of the rules and restrictions that might impact you.

Visas

To obtain a tourist visa for Japan, you need a passport with at least six months of validity left and at least two blank pages. For citizens of 68 countries (including the United States, Canada, United Kingdom, Australia, New Zealand and most of Europe), no visa application will be required. Once you get to Japan, your passport is stamped, and that is the start of your 90-day tourist visa.

To see Japan's visa requirements and who will need to submit an application prior to arriving, you can check out the Japan National Tourism Organization (JNTO) information page at https://www.japan.travel/en/plan/visa-info.

Customs and Prohibited Items

Bringing weapons into Japan is prohibited. This obviously means firearms (which are illegal in Japan), but also includes pocketknives and multi-tools with blades. Customs is very strict about enforcement, so be sure to double-check your belongings prior to leaving home.

Medications and Controlled Substances

Japan has a zero tolerance policy for illegal narcotics and street drugs. They also have very specific regulations about medications. In fact, some medications that are perfectly legal in other countries are prohibited in Japan (and several often-prescribed ADHD medications, as well as over-the-counter antihistamines containing pseudoephedrine, are on the prohibited list).

There are also certain medicines you'll need to apply for permission to bring, so be sure to check the Japan Ministry of Health, Labor and Welfare website well in advance of your travel. Go to www.mhlw.go.jp for more information.

Pets and Service Animals

Pets and animals are subject to strict quarantine, with the exception of certified and properly vetted service animals. Be sure to check the requirements and prepare well in advance of your trip if you plan to bring an animal with you to Japan.

Your Passport

Japanese law requires you carry your passport with you at all times. Japanese law also requires that hotels copy your passport as part of the check-in process.

Pro Tip

The JR Yamanote Line (color-coded green) is one of Japan's busiest rail lines. It makes a big loop around Tokyo, with a total of 29 stops. While Yamanote will get you just about anywhere you want to go in Tokyo, it may not be your best option if you want to get somewhere quickly, as it takes about an hour to make the full loop.

If time is a concern, or you want to get to the other side of Tokyo without making the loop, check to see if the JR Chuo Line will work for you. It runs east-west through the middle of Tokyo and offers a rapid service (color-coded orange). The yellow-coded Chuo line makes more stops.

Health & Safety

Japan's health and safety statistics are very good. Most travelers don't have any issues, but it's always good to know what to do in case you do run into a problem.

Health Standards

Japan's standards of health are very high. Tap water is safe to drink and food-handling regulations are strict, so food and water-borne illnesses are rarely a concern for travelers.

Hospitals and Medical Care

Japanese hospitals are modern and doctors are highly trained. Medical treatment is provided by universal healthcare to citizens and residents, but it's not free for tourists. In fact, Japanese medical bills can be quite hefty, so you may consider getting travel insurance.

Another thing to note is that while many hospitals have bilingual staff, not all do, so there could be a language barrier. If this happens, you can either reach out to your embassy or consulate, or to Japan Medical Service Accreditation for International Patients (JMIP) for assistance. You can read more about JMIP at jmip.jme.or.jp.

Crime and Law Enforcement

Japan has one of the lowest overall crime rates in the world. The most frequently reported crimes against tourists are theft-related incidents like pickpocketing (though even these incidents are relatively rare). If you are the victim of a crime, report it to the police and to your consulate or embassy. They can help you with next steps.

The emergency number for police is 1-1-**0**. Police personnel can also be found in police boxes (*kōban*) in most neighborhoods. Look for the little building with the red light over the door.

Natural Disasters

Japan is subject to natural disasters just like anywhere else. Typhoon season is from May-October, and peaks in August and September. Earthquakes (and the tsunamis they cause) can happen at any time.

The Japanese Government provides English language disaster and weather alerts and information through a "J-Alert". You can get J-Alerts in English by downloading the NHK World app. The Japan Meteorological Agency (JMA) also has an English language website that shows all active alerts for Japan. You can check it out at www.jmo.go.jp/jma/indexe.html.

Another option is to set up disaster alerts on your Apple device by going into Settings and turning on Alerts. See Apple Support for more information on how it works and how to set it up.

Getting Help

The emergency phone number for ambulance services and the fire department is 1-1-**9**.

The Japanese phrase for "I need help" is *Tasuke ga hitsuyōdesu* (pronounced ta sū kay ga heet sū yo dess).

> ****Pro Tip****
> Not all ATMs accept overseas cards, but those at convenience stores and post offices usually do. For any withdrawals you make, ATMs will give you the current exchange rate and charge a small transaction fee.

Basic Japanese Culture Tips

Japan is a group culture based on hospitality and convenience. While many aspects of Japanese culture are similar to western culture, there are some uniquely Japanese customs that are good to know.

Bowing

Bowing is used to communicate. It's the customary greeting in Japan and is also how you say thank you and I'm sorry. If someone bows to you, it's polite to return the gesture. While bows vary greatly depending on the circumstances, a 45-degree angle bend at the waist usually works pretty well. Being a foreigner, you won't be judged on your technique.

Shoe Removal

Be sure to remove your shoes if you enter a private home, the inner rooms of a temple, or any floor covered in a straw mat (*tatami*). In general, raised floors inside a building mean it's time to remove your shoes. Shoes are left in the entryway or outside the door and are neatly placed facing out (so you can slide your feet right in when you return).

In public places, slippers are often provided for you to wear after you remove your shoes. Be sure to take them off prior to going back outside. (It's also a good idea to have clean socks!)

Train Etiquette

Most travelers notice right away how quiet Japanese train cars are. This is because talking can disturb other passengers and that's a no-no in Japanese culture. You will probably see some exceptions, particularly with children, but overall, most passengers observe the quiet rule. If you must talk, try and whisper and make it quick.

Cell phone etiquette in Japan is also a bit more strict than what many are used to. It's considered rude to talk on your cell phone while on the train. (It's fine to use your phone for other things like texting or playing games, just be sure it's on silent mode.)

The long-distance shinkansen are a little different. While you still shouldn't talk on your phone in the cars, it's okay to make a call if you step into the space between cars near the exit, because it's separate from the passengers and you won't disturb anyone.

Walk and Drive on the Left Side
In Japan, you walk on the left side of the sidewalk and stairs (unless otherwise indicated), and when standing on the escalator, be sure to stand to the left so others who are in a hurry can pass. You also drive on the left in Japan.

Slurping Noodles
This is common practice in Japan. While not everyone does it, it's perfectly normal and not considered rude. In fact, slurping in Japan signals enjoyment, helps prevent the broth from splashing, and helps cool the noodles as you eat them. So if you want to slurp, go ahead!

Chopsticks Etiquette

Never leave your chopsticks stuck in the rice as this symbolizes death. Instead, place the chopsticks on the chopstick rest or lay them across your plate/bowl. Also, if you need to make hand gestures during mealtime conversation, set your chopsticks down first. Don't wave them around in your hand while talking because it's considered bad manners.

If you find you're unable to use chopsticks, it's totally fine to ask for western-style utensils, just be aware they may not have them available.

A Word About Tattoos

In Japan, tattoos are associated with the Yakuza organized crime group, and among the Japanese, Yakuza members are usually the only people that have them. Tattoos were also previously used to mark a criminal instead of carrying out a death sentence, so tattoos have a pretty deeply-rooted negative history in Japan.

Because of this, many public bath houses (*onsen*) have a strict "no tattoos" rule. Some may look the other way for a westerner, but most don't, so if you have tattoos, it's best to find an onsen that allows them.

One of the most popular tattoo-friendly spots is Hakone Yumoto Onsen (KAI Hakone), located in the hot spring resort town of Hakone. In fact, Hoshino Resorts (who owns the onsen) has many locations throughout Japan and all allow tattoos (you just have to cover them with complimentary stickers). You can check out their website at <u>hoshi-noresorts.com</u>.

Natural Hot Spring Hisamatsuyu is another great tattoo-friendly onsen, and they have locations in the Sakuradai and Ikebukuro areas of Tokyo (and no stickers are required.) You can check them out at <u>http://hisamatsuyu.jp</u>.

<u>Pro Tip</u>

Tipping (gratuity) is not customary in Japan and is neither required nor expected. In fact, if you do tip, you may cause confusion. Therefore, the best thing to do to reward great service in Japan is simply express your thanks. To do this, you can bow and say *Arigatou* (pronounced ah-ree-ga-toh), which means thank you in Japanese.

Answers to Frequently Asked Questions From First Time Travelers to Japan

Answers to
Frequently Asked Questions
From First Time Travelers to Japan

Traveling to a country for the first time is exciting, and it's normal to have questions. Some things you'll just have to find out for yourself (and that's part of the fun), but other questions can be answered prior to your travel and can even help you plan your trip.

Is it hard to get around if I don't speak the language?

While Japanese is generally considered a difficult language to learn, memorizing a few phrases and using a phrasebook are easy and will go a long way. Japan also posts signs for just about everything, and those signs often have English translations. While English language signs are less common in smaller towns, many travelers still find the signs' pictures helpful.

You can also usually find excellent English language assistance at JR ticket offices and with front desk staff in large hotels. If all else fails, you can use gestures or draw a picture. While these methods are rudimentary, they tend to cross language barriers well.

Do the Japanese like foreigners?

The Japanese are a very welcoming and friendly people. In fact, one of the fundamentals of Japanese culture is hospitality (called *omotenashi*), and going above and beyond to help someone is the norm. While you may notice some Japanese seem a bit uncomfortable around foreigners, it's usually because they're worried about their English-speaking skills.

Most travelers report excellent customer service experiences and usually, if someone can't help you they'll find somebody who can.

What are Airport Security, Immigration & Customs like in Japan?

In comparison to other countries, Japanese Airport Security, Immigration and Customs seem organized and efficient, and lines usually move pretty quickly. At Customs, the officer will ask where you're staying and may want to look in your luggage.

At Immigration, you turn in your visa application (which will be provided to you on the plane and must be filled out **prior to** approaching the officer). They'll also stamp your passport and take your fingerprints at Immigration.

Airport security lines are usually pretty short and you won't need to remove your shoes unless specifically asked. Like most other places, liquids and gels will need to be passed through the scanner in a small, clear, plastic bag.

You can check Narita Airport's English language website www.narita-airport.jp for more details on travel rules and regulations. You can find English language information for Haneda Airport at tokyo-haneda.com.

How is the food and how will I know what to order?

As a rule, Japanese food is fantastic. There a huge number of dining options, and the Japanese are adamant about freshness, cleanliness and good presentation. So you're likely to find a great meal just about anywhere you go. While there are some unusual foods in Japan, you'll be able to find more familiar options if that's what you prefer. Not only you will see western fast food chains, there are usually western-style foods available in department store food halls.

Ordering food is usually pretty easy too. Many Japanese restaurants have realistic plastic versions of the dishes they serve in their front windows and these displays are often numbered. So if you decide you want to order a particular item, you can just find its number on the menu and show your server.

Even if there are no plastic displays at the restaurant entrance, Japanese menus usually have pictures of their most popular dishes, so you can just point to what you want.

Is taking photographs okay?

The majority of the time, taking pictures is no problem in Japan. There are some exceptions though, like at markets and temples. In markets, you'll see seafood and produce not found anywhere else in the world and will understandably want to take a picture. Photos aren't usually an issue if you just ask first, and sometimes the vendor will even pose for you. Just ask, get the okay, and snap away. (You can probably just point to your camera and they'll figure it out.)

At temples, you can take pictures of the grounds and building exteriors, but pictures of the main hall where worship takes place are often prohibited. Signs are usually posted if this is the case.

I want to mail souvenirs home. How is the Japanese postal system?

In Japan, the postal system is very efficient and reliable. Letterboxes and post offices (*yūbinkyoku*) are plentiful and easily recognizable (both are marked with what appears to be a red capital T with a line over it). Be aware though, that the international mailing rates for boxes can be pricey.

If you do decide to mail something, you'll need to fill out a detailed form listing the contents. As with any postal system, hazardous items are not allowed, and in Japan, this includes batteries (and if you have toys on your packing list, post office staff will probably ask you if they have batteries).

You can pay by cash or card in most post offices, and you'll get a tracking number for any parcels you send.

Will my cell phone and electronic devices work, and will I have internet access?

The majority of foreign cell phones aren't fully functional in Japan. The texting function usually works (but watch out for data charges). If you need to have a working cell phone and yours isn't cooperating, get a disposable phone. Wireless providers usually have small stores or kiosks in airports and large train stations.

If you just want to make calls home, you can try a Voice Over Internet Protocol (VoIP), which allows you to make calls over the internet. Whatsapp is a popular choice, and LINE is the most popular VoIP in Japan (and both are free). Just be sure both you and the person you want to talk to have the app installed prior to your travel.

Electronic devices like tablets and computers work exactly the same in Japan as they do anywhere else – they need a power supply and an internet connection. If you find that internet connectivity is a problem, you can rent a portable pocket Wi-Fi, usually pretty cheaply. They're available at most airports and large train stations, or, you can rent one when/if you purchase a JR Pass (for an additional fee).

Free Wi-Fi is pretty common in Tokyo and large cities, but less so in smaller towns. You can typically access free Wi-Fi at most airports, train stations, Starbucks and 7-Eleven convenience stores (but note that 7-Eleven and Starbucks require you to register first and you may need a translation tool for their sign up pages).

Tokyo is huge. How can I figure out where to go and not get lost?

Tokyo is one of the largest cities in the world. So it's understandable you might worry about how to navigate it, especially with a language barrier.

Luckily, Tokyo is laid out relatively simply. The city is divided into wards, and a great way to remember which ward is located where is to look at a map of the Yamanote rail line (color-coded green; symbol JY). It makes a big loop around Tokyo and stops at most of the places tourists want to go. Google Maps usually has Japan's landmarks (including train stations) in English as well.

 Even if you do get lost, Tokyo is literally packed with train stations. So you'll probably find one after a short walk and you can go inside and use the maps to get back on track. If for some reason you don't see a station, you can always hail a taxi (they're actually pretty easy to get) and ask them to take you to the nearest station, or your destination. An available taxi will show a red light on the front dash and roof, whereas a green light means the taxi is currently hired and not available.

If you want to ask for directions to the nearest train station, you can just say "eki" (pronounced eh-kee) with a question inflection, and the person you're asking will probably figure out what you mean.

How do I use the Japanese rail system and can I pre-pay my fare?

Japan's rail system is very efficient, and has excellent safety and on-time records. It's also the most popular mode of public transportation in Japan. With the exception of rural areas, you'll usually have several options to get to your destination.

Using the trains is also pretty easy. Each rail line has its own color and letter, making it easy to find on maps, and those maps are prominently posted in stations (usually above the ticket machines). You can also find rail maps online, along with train timetables and station maps. Fares for each stop are also shown on rail maps.

If you don't want to figure out your fare every time you travel, you can purchase a Pasmo or Suica card. You simply purchase one of these cards at a train station vending machine, load money onto it, then swipe it at the ticket turnstiles. (Note that there is a small fee for the card and neither Pasmo nor Suica can be used for the shinkansen.) Ticket machines and pre-paid fare card vending machines both have an English language option.

Many trains stations in Tokyo have both JR and Tokyo Metro trains (the most commonly used services), but sometimes they're separate. Usually, Tokyo Metro and JR stations are located fairly close together (and you can often access them by a tunnel or covered walkway when they're separate.) Tokyo also has rail lines run by Toei, Keisei and Seibu, but these are less common.

You can get maps for stations served by JR trains at www.jreast.co/jp/e/stations. You can get Tokyo Metro station maps at www.tokyometro.jp.

Pro Tip

In Japanese, Hello is Konnichiwa (pronounced *kon-nee-chee-wah*).
Goodbye is Sayounara (pronounced *sah-yo-na-ra*).
Please is Kudasai (pronounced *koo-dah-sah-ee*).

Helpful Links

Bay Hotel capsule hotel for women in Akihabara, Tokyo - **www.bay-hotel.jp**

Ebisu Dedusuke izakaya in Tokyo - **dedesuke.com**

Ebisu Kura izakaya in Tokyo - **ebisu-kura.com**

Ganso Zushi conveyor belt sushi restaurant locations and info - **gansozushi.com**

Haneda Airport maps and travel information - **tokyo-haneda.com**

Hoshino Resorts tattoo-friendly onsen - **www.hoshinoresorts.com/en**

Japan Meteorological Agency (JMA) alerts - **www.jmo.go.jp/jma/indexe.html**

Japanalytic travel blog - **www.japanalytic.com**

Jetstar discount airlines - **www.jetstar.com**

JMIP international patient assistance and information - **jmip.jme.or.jp**

JNTO visa information - **https://www.japan.travel/en/plan/visa-info**

JR Pass - **jrailpass.com**

JR train station maps - **www.jreast.co/jp/e/stations**

Kyoto Station map and information - **www.kyotostation.com**

Matsumoto Castle in Nagano - **matsumoto-castle.jp**

Medication restrictions and applications for permission - **www.mhlw.go.jp**

Mount Fuji trail and volcanic alert information - **www.fujisan-climb.jp**

Mount Takao - **www.japan.travel/en/itineraries/mt-takao-a-mountain-filled-with-surprises**

Narita Airport maps and travel information - **www.narita-airport.jp**

Natural Hot Spring Hisamatsuyu tattoo-friendly onsen - **http://hisamatsuyu.jp**

Nine Hours capsule hotel for women in Shinjuku, Tokyo - **ninehours.co.jp**

Nishiki Market, Kyoto information - **kyoto-nishiki.or.jp**

Peach discount airlines - **www.flypeach.com**

Sapporo Station information - **www.sapporostation.com**

Senso-ji Temple in Asakusa, Tokyo - **senso-ji.jp**

Shuri Castle Park in Naha, Okinawa - **oki-park.jp**

Skymark discount airlines - **www.skymark.co.jp**

Solamachi shops and restaurants, Tokyo - **www.tokyo-solamachi.jp**

Takashimaya department store information - **takashimaya-global.com**

Tokyo Metro station maps - **www.tokyometro.jp**

Toyosu Fish Market information - **toyosu-market.or.jp**

Yasaka Shrine, Kyoto information - **yasaka-jinja.or.jp**

Read More About Japan & Get Helpful Tips

Want more Japan? Need travel suggestions? Then check out the Japanalytic™ travel blog. There are posts on Japanese culture, food and entertainment, as well as helpful posts about where to go and what to do while you're there.

Read more at **www.japanalytic.com**.

Follow Us!

You can also follow Japanalytic™ on social media. We post daily!

- Instagram: **@japanalytic**
- Facebook: **facebook.com/japanalytic**

Coming Soon

Look for more Japanalytic™ travel books, coming soon! Topics include:
- Japanese Culture
- Japanese Food
- Doing Business in Japan
- What to Do in Tokyo
- What to Do in Kyoto
- Best Day Trips from Tokyo

Made in United States
North Haven, CT
18 December 2023